I0493391

101 Quotes
To Think
And
Grow Rich

Curated By
Donna Still

Cover Design: Donna Still www.donnastill.com
Book Design: Ultimate Life Publishing,
www.donnastill.com
Book Production: Create Space an www.amazon.com
company

First published in Great Britain 2017

Legal Disclaimer

Published by kind permission of The Napoleon Hill
Foundation who currently hold all copyrights for the
works of Napoleon Hill. www.naphill.org

Dedication

I dedicate this book to all the seekers of truth; those who are prepared to set aside their beliefs and trust in a greater power to do their bidding.

Bless your hearts

Authors preface

As with all material of a personal development nature, nothing happens unless you implement the strategies and apply them directly into your life. When I began implementing the strategies consistently in my life changes were so dramatic that the people around me no longer recognised any of my behaviours. It made them uncomfortable at first but over time they have grown to realise that if you really want anything in life then its up to you to do what ever it takes to achieve it. That's why I believe Napoleon Hills work was so powerfully ahead of its time. His work is also based on 25 years of practical research and literally gives you the tools, the rest is up to you.

Introduction

Since being introduced the work of Napoleon Hill by my mentor Bob Proctor, I can honestly say that it has impacted every area of my life in a huge and very positive way. From the way I interact with my grandchildren, family and colleagues to the amount of money now in my bank account, there isn't one area I'm happy to say that has not been positively affected.

My purpose for curating the content in this book is to ensure the timeless wisdom of Napoleon Hill is accessible to a new generation through bite-sized and social media friendly sized quotes that convey the original intention of the full book.

Think and Grow Rich was originally published in 1937. Since publication it has gone on to be one of the most respected business books ever written and has sold over 70 million copies according to Forbes magazine. I hope you get as much out of it as I did when I began reading and implementing the information.
There have been many well known business men, women and authors who all accredit their success to the founding principles Hill wrote about and published all those years ago.

I have followed the original book layout for the chapters and each chapter contains quotes from the original text that will insure an understanding of what I believe is the essence the author originally wanted to convey. I hope you enjoy it as much as I have in curating the content and wish you every success in implementing the strategies and achieving the riches you so deservedly desire.
Fortune favour's the courageous so get stuck in, apply the principles and you'll never want for anything ever again because as Hill said,

"Riches when they come are never the result of hard work! Riches come if they come at all in response to definite demands, based upon the application of definite principles and not by chance or luck."

"You can build a fortune using natures immutable laws – but first you must understand the laws"

That is exactly what this book gives you ~ A brief overview of the principles to begin your own journey towards riches and further study.

Chapter One

Desire

~

The starting point of ALL achievement: The First step toward riches

1. "More gold has been mined from the brains of men than has ever been taken from the earth"

2. "Desire is a thought impulse – thought impulses are forms of energy"

3. "We have the power to control our thoughts"

4. "Adopt a definite purpose and stand by that purpose until it has become an all consuming passion"

5. "I will burn all bridges behind me and stake my entire future on my ability to get what I want"

6. "Only those who become money conscious ever achieve great riches"

7. "Every great leader from the dawn of civilization down to the present was a dreamer"

8. "Practical dreamers have always been the pattern makers of civilization"

9. "There is a difference between wishing for a thing and being ready to receive it. No one is ready for a thing until he believes he can acquire it"

10. "Remember, no more effort is required to aim high and demand prosperity and abundance than is required to accept misery poverty and lack"

11. "A burning desire has devious ways of transmuting itself into its physical equivalent"

Chapter Two

Faith

~

Visualisation of and belief in attainment of desire:
The second step towards riches

12. "Faith is a state of mind you can develop at will…
Faith is a state of mind that may be induced by self
suggestion"

13. "Faith is the eternal elixir which gives life, power and action to the impulse of thought."

14. "Nothing is impossible to the man who backs burning desire with enduring faith"

15. "All thoughts that have been emotionalised (given feeling) and mixed with faith, begin immediately to translate themselves into their physical counterpart."

16. "Perfection will come through practice. It cannot come by merely reading instructions."

17. "When the opportunity came, it appeared in a different form, and from a different direction"

18. "Initiative, faith and the will to win are three intangible forces available to man"

19. "Faith is the basis of all miracles and mysteries which cannot be analysed by the rules of science."

20. "Faith is the only known antidote to failure"

Chapter Three

Auto Suggestion

~

The Medium For Influencing the Subconscious Mind: The Third Step towards Riches

21. No thought, whether it be negative or positive, can enter the subconscious mind without the aid of auto suggestion"

22. "Everything which man creates begins in the form of a thought impulse"

23. "Any idea, plan or purpose placed in the mind through repetition of thought

24. "Every man is what he is because of the dominating thoughts he permits to occupy his mind"

25. "The law of auto suggestion will lead you into peace and prosperity or down into the valley of misery, failure and death according to your application of i

26. "An educated person is the one who has so developed the faculties of their mind that they can acquire anything they want or its equivalent"

27. "Knowledge has no value except that which can be gained from its application to some worthy end"

28. "Successful men in all callings, never stop acquiring specialised knowledge related to their major purpose, business or profession"

29. "The close association with those who refuse to compromise with circumstances he does not like is an asset that can never be measured in terms of money"

Chapter Five

Imagination

~

The Workshop of The Mind:
The Fifth Step Towards Riches

30. "There is no standard price on ideas. The creator of ideas makes his own price and if he's smart – GETS IT"

31. "Ideas are the beginning point for ALL great fortunes"

32. "Man can create nothing that he does not first conceive in thought"

33. "Through the aid of imagination, thought impulses become assembled into plans"

34. "Nothing can stand in the way of imagination mixed with faith"

35. "If you cannot see great riches in your mind you will never see them in your bank account"

36. "Any person may rise to heights of achievement which stagger the imagination"

37. "Ideas are intangible forces, but they have more power than the physical brains that give birth to them"

38. "Ideas have the power to live on longer than the brain that created them has turned to dust"

Chapter Six

Organised Planning

~

The Crystalisation of Desire Into Action: The Sixth Step Toward Riches

39. "Knowledge only becomes power when it is organised into definite plans of action and directed to a definite end"

40. "No man is ever whipped until he quits – in his own mind"

41. "Money of itself is just inert matter, it cannot move, think or talk, but it can hear when a person who desires it comes to call"

42. "The world does not pay men for what they know, it pays them for what they do, or induce others to do with what they know"

Chapter Seven

Decision

~

The Mystery of Procrastination: The Seventh Step Towards riches

43. "Definiteness of decisions always requires great courage"

44. "Men who succeed reach decisions promptly, and change them if at all slowly. Men who fail, reach decisions slowly and change them frequently"

45. "Self mastery is the hardest job you will ever tackle. If you do not conquer self, you'll be conquered by self"

46. "Opinions are the cheapest commodity on earth. Everyone has a flock of them ready to be wished upon anyone who will accept them"

47. "The eternal laws of nature are available to anyone who has the faith and courage to use them"

48. "The world has a habit of making room for the person who's words and actions shows that he knows where he's going"

Chapter Eight

Persistence

~

The Sustained Effort Necessary to Induce Faith: The Eighth Step Towards Riches

49. "Persistence is an essential factor in the procedure of transmuting desire into its monetary equivalent"

50. "Whenever great men and women have acquired riches you can be sure they first acquired persistence"

51. "Keep on keeping on, no matter how hard it appears"

52. "Our only limitations are those we set up in our own minds"

53. "Will power and desire when properly combined make an irresistible pair"

54. "Riches do not respond to wishes, they respond to definite plans, backed by definite desires through constant persistence"

Chapter Nine

Power Of The Master Mind

~

The Driving Force: The Ninth Step Towards Riches

55. "Economic advantages may be created by any person who surrounds himself with the advice, counsel and personal co operation of a group of men who are willing to lend him wholehearted aid in the spirit of perfect harmony"

56. "Analyse the record of any person who has accumulated a great fortune and many of those who have accumulated modest fortunes and you will find that either consciously or unconsciously employed the master mind principle. Great power can be accumulated through no other principle"

57. "Energy is natures universal set of building blocks, out of which she constructs every material thing in the universe, including man and every form of animal and vegetable life"

58. "When a group of individual brains are co ordinated and function in harmony, the increased energy created through that alliance becomes available to every kind of brain in the group"

59. "Men take on the nature, the habits and the power of thought of those whom they associate in the spirit of sympathy and harmony"

60. "When riches take the place of poverty, the change is usually brought about through well conceived and carefully executed plans. Poverty needs no plan"

Chapter Ten

The Mystery Of Sex

~

Transmutation: The Tenth step towards Riches

61. "Sex desire (Passion) is the most powerful of all human desires, when driven by desire/passion a person develops a keenness of imagination, courage, will power, persistence and creative ability unknown in other times"

62. "When driven by the passion and desire of creative expression, one pulls in resources to form a super human power for action"

63. "Definition of a genius – A person who has discovered how to increase the vibrations of thought to the point where he can freely communicate with sources of knowledge not available through the ordinary vibration of thought"

64. "Genius is developed through the sixth sense – creative imagination"

65. "The faculty of the creative imagination is the direct link between the finite mind of man and infinite intelligence"

66. "The creative faculty of the mind is set into action by emotion"

67. "The emotion of love brings out and develops the artistic nature of a person"

68. "The secret of self control lies in understanding the process of transmutation"

Chapter Eleven

The Sub Conscious Mind

~

The Connecting Link: The Eleventh Step towards riches

69. "The sub conscious mind consists of a field of consciousness in which every impulse of thought that reaches the objective mind through any of the five senses is classified and recorded, and from which thoughts may be recalled or withdrawn as if a letter taken from a filing cabinet"

70. "The subconscious mind acts first on the dominating desires which have been mixed with the emotional feeling such as faith"

71. "The subconscious works night and day"

72. "The subconscious mind contains the secret process by which mental impulses are modified and changed into their spiritual equivalent"

73. "The subconscious mind is the medium of communication between the thinking mind of man and infinite intelligence"

74. "The mind is a creature of habit. It thrives upon the dominating thoughts fed it. Through the faculty of will power"

75. "The subconscious mind will not remain idle! If you fail to plant desires in your subconscious mind, it will feed upon the thoughts that reach it as a result of your neglect"

76. "Control of the mind through will power is not difficult. Control comes through persistence and habit"

77. "The subconscious mind will translate into reality a thought driven by fear just as readily as it will translate into reality a thought driven by courage"

78. "Thoughts are truly things, for the reason that every material thing begins in the form of thought energy"

79. "Positive and negative emotions cannot occupy at the same time. One or the other must dominate"

www.donnastill.com

Chapter Twelve

The Brain

~

A Broadcasting And Receiving Station For Thought:
The Twelfth Step Towards Riches

80. "Every human being is capable of picking up vibrations of thought released by other brains"

81. "The creative imagination is the receiving set of the brain"

Chapter Thirteen

The Sixth Sense

~

The Door To The Temple Of Wisdom: The Thirteenth Step Towards Riches

82. "The sixth sense is the faculty which marks the difference between a genius and an ordinary individual. This faculty can be cultivated and developed through use"

83. "Understanding the sixth sense comes only by meditation"

84. "There comes to your aid a guardian angel who will open to you at all times the door of the temple of wisdom"

85. "Nature never deviates from established laws"

86. "There is a power, or first cause, or intelligence, which permeates every atom of matter, and embraces every unit of energy perceivable to man – that is infinite intelligence"

Bonus Chapter

How to outwit The Six Ghosts Of Fear

~

Take Inventory Of Yourself

87. "Before we can master an enemy – we must know its name – FEAR. Fears are nothing more than states of mind. Ones states of mind is subject to control and direction"

88. "Nature has endowed man with absolute control over but one thing, and that is thought"

89. "A state of mind is something that one assumes"

90. "Criticism builds fear in the human heart"

91. "Both energy and matter can be transformed, but neither can be destroyed"

Final Thoughts
To Remember For Your Continued Success

92. "An unsettled mind is helpless"

93. "Indecision makes an unsettled mind"

94. "Mental telepathy is a reality – whether this fact is recognised or not by either the person releasing the thoughts or the person receiving the thoughts"

95. "You are the master of your own earthly destiny just as surely as you have the power to control your own thoughts"

96. "If you fail to control your own mind you may be sure that you will control nothing else"

97. "You may influence, direct and eventually control your own environment, making your life exactly as you want it to be"

98. "Mind control is the result of self discipline and habit, you either control your mind or it controls you"

99. "Every thought you have is like an arrow and a magnet"

100. "Your mind is your spiritual estate"

101. "Make your life to order"

Afterword

With this content in your hands you really have no excuses for not loving your life and living it fully. What ever comes your way is really only a stepping-stone to that which you do want. Firstly though, like Hill says you must be clear on what it is you want, otherwise how can the universe provide it for you? Secondly trusting that every event is a stepping-stone taking you towards that which you hold In your heart is what Hill describes as faith. True faith holds the capacity for you to transcend apparent circumstances and look at the bigger picture. As always hindsight is an amazing tool.

Acknowledgements

I'd like to thank so many people but the pages are too small for that so I'm going to honour those who played a part in getting this information out to the world.

To begin with those who have helped me discover my true self and take control of my own mind so that source can do it's work through me. When we get out of the way and stop blocking our good the ease and flow that follows is astounding. So the first person to thank is Napoleon Hill himself for being courageous enough to share his work with the world in such an impactful way. The Napoleon hill Foundation for their support in developing this book, and more specifically Don Green whose dedication to the cause is profoundly humbling. I'd like to thank Bob Proctor for so generously sharing his own insights gained scientifically through more than 50 years of intense study into Hills material that ignited a fire in my soul to find out more and dive much deeper into my own consciousness. And sincere thanks to Sandra Gallagher for developing the Thinking Into results Program that really did change the way I viewed the world. I'd also like to thank Amanda Holges, Deborah Mulvany, Caroline Love and the members at Metis Women for their clarity, their wisdom their unconditional support and encouragement during the process of curating this content early in 2016. And finally I'd like to thank my good friend and fellow spiritual adventurer Matthew Griffin for the endless conversations and discussions on many of the principles and quotes in this book and the truth behind their original meaning and how to apply them now in this moment.

Thank YOU for being such bright lights in my life. ☺

The Proctor Gallagher Institute
www.proctorgallagherinstitute.com

The Purpose and mission of the Proctor Gallagher Institute

"Our vision is to significantly improve the quality of lives globally by elevating the quality of thoughts individually.

We do this by educating and empowering our audience through products, services and events that expand awareness and harmonize people with the natural, immutable Laws of the Universe.

We intend to play a significant role in creating a world in which true wealth—spiritual, material, intellectual—flows to, through and from every person in an ever-expanding, never-ending cycle of abundance."

Check out their website for courses and events in a town near you. Or check out my website www.donnastill.com for events, courses and training in this material.

The Napoleon Hill Foundation
www.naphill.org

The purpose and mission of The Napoleon Hill Foundation

"The Napoleon Hill Foundation is a nonprofit educational institution dedicated to making the world a better place in which to live"

Next Steps

I would recommend experimenting with this material as it really does have the power to help you change the course of your life. If you'd like someone to guide you on this journey of experimentation then contact me through www.donnastill.com or join my facebook community. You can find me by typing in the Diamond Detective

About The Author
Donna Still
www.donnastill.com

Donna Still, the Diamond Detective is the author of 15 books. 3 published Ditch the Scales, The Art Of Effective Communication In A Digital World & The Divine Nature Of Being and 12 up and coming, all in the genre of creating a better life by exposing what's already within. A creator of programs that cause massive change and transformation by providing tools and training to communicate, think, live and practice from a place of self love, self trust and authentic, spontaneous creativity.

Donna is a specialist personal & business performance consultant and works with small and medium sized businesses to get them working in flow and playing a much bigger game for a sustainable business legacy. Donna believes that mastery of the mind is the route to liberation and freedom from what holds people back in their life and business. She is an avid reader and devourer of personal and business development material, an eternal student and leader, scouring libraries and attending training programs to find the best tools to help others to simplify their life and live it on their terms, while making a difference in the world.

Further Reading

The following authors provide additional understanding to the topics covered by the quotes in this book and will help you in understanding the ideas and concepts that support Hills original work.

Think & Grow Rich	Napoleon Hill
The Science Of Getting Rich	Wallace D Wattles
You Were Born Rich	Bob Proctor
Working With The Laws	Raymond Holliwell
Open Your Mind To Prosperity	Catherine Ponder
The Prosperity Secrets Of The Ages	Catherine Ponder
The Power Of Awareness	Neville Goddard
E squared	Pam Grout
The Secret	Rhonda Byrne
Lead The Field	Earl Nightingale
Wishes Fulfilled	Dr Wayne Dyer
Psycho Cybernetics	Maxwell Maltz